50 Desserts in a Jar
Recipes for Home

By: Kelly Johnson

Table of Contents

- Chocolate Mousse
- Strawberry Shortcake
- Key Lime Pie
- Tiramisu
- Cookie Dough Parfait
- Brownie Sundae
- S'mores in a Jar
- Lemon Curd Tart
- Pumpkin Cheesecake
- Red Velvet Cake
- Panna Cotta
- Apple Crisp
- Peanut Butter Pie
- Cheesecake Brownies
- Berry Trifle
- Mocha Pudding
- Coconut Cream Pie
- Rice Pudding
- Chocolate Chip Cookie Pie
- Mango Sticky Rice
- Nutella Mousse
- Chocolate Lava Cake
- Banana Pudding
- Carrot Cake
- Matcha Parfait
- Oreo Cheesecake
- Cherry Clafoutis
- Almond Joy Parfait
- Tarte Tatin
- Zucchini Bread Pudding
- Saffron Rice Pudding
- Snickerdoodle Parfait
- Coconut Macaroon Jars
- Funfetti Cake
- Chocolate Peanut Butter Pie

- Fruit Salad with Honey Yogurt
- Mini Pavlova
- Chocolate Tart
- Dulce de Leche Flan
- Lemon Blueberry Trifle
- Gingerbread Cake
- Chocolate Biscotti Parfait
- Blackberry Fool
- Pistachio Pudding
- Strawberry Rhubarb Crumble
- Vanilla Bean Pudding
- Cookie Butter Cups
- White Chocolate Raspberry Cheesecake
- Chai-Spiced Rice Pudding
- Chocolate Almond Torte

Chocolate Mousse

Ingredients

- **1 cup** dark chocolate, chopped
- **2 cups** heavy cream
- **3 tbsp** sugar
- **1 tsp** vanilla extract
- **Pinch of salt**

Instructions

1. **Melt Chocolate**: Melt the chocolate in a double boiler and let cool slightly.
2. **Whip Cream**: In a separate bowl, whip the cream, sugar, vanilla, and salt until soft peaks form.
3. **Combine**: Fold the melted chocolate into the whipped cream until smooth. Refrigerate for at least 2 hours before serving.

Strawberry Shortcake

Ingredients

- **2 cups** strawberries, sliced
- **¼ cup** sugar
- **2 cups** whipped cream
- **4 shortcake biscuits**

Instructions

1. **Prepare Strawberries**: Toss strawberries with sugar and let sit for 30 minutes.
2. **Assemble**: Split the biscuits, layer with strawberries and whipped cream, and top with more strawberries.

Key Lime Pie

Ingredients

- **1 cup** key lime juice
- **1 can (14 oz)** sweetened condensed milk
- **3 large egg yolks**
- **1 graham cracker crust**
- **Lime slices**, for garnish

Instructions

1. **Mix Filling**: In a bowl, whisk together key lime juice, sweetened condensed milk, and egg yolks until smooth.
2. **Bake**: Pour into the crust and bake at 350°F (175°C) for about 15 minutes. Chill before serving and garnish with lime slices.

Tiramisu

Ingredients

- **1 cup** strong brewed coffee, cooled
- **2 tbsp** coffee liqueur (optional)
- **1 cup** mascarpone cheese
- **1 cup** heavy cream
- **¼ cup** sugar
- **24 ladyfinger cookies**
- **Cocoa powder**, for dusting

Instructions

1. **Combine Coffee**: Mix brewed coffee with liqueur in a shallow dish.
2. **Whip Cream**: In a bowl, whip cream and sugar until soft peaks form. Fold in mascarpone.
3. **Layer**: Dip ladyfingers in coffee and layer in a dish. Spread mascarpone mixture over, repeating layers. Chill for at least 4 hours and dust with cocoa before serving.

Cookie Dough Parfait

Ingredients

- **1 cup** cookie dough (edible version, no eggs)
- **2 cups** whipped cream
- **½ cup** chocolate chips

Instructions

1. **Layer Ingredients**: In a glass, layer cookie dough, whipped cream, and chocolate chips.
2. **Repeat**: Continue layering until the glass is full, finishing with whipped cream and chocolate chips on top.

Brownie Sundae

Ingredients

- **2 cups** brownie bites (store-bought or homemade)
- **2 cups** vanilla ice cream
- **Chocolate syrup** for drizzling
- **Chopped nuts** for topping
- **Whipped cream** (optional)

Instructions

1. **Assemble Sundae**: In a bowl, layer brownie bites and vanilla ice cream.
2. **Top**: Drizzle with chocolate syrup, add nuts, and whipped cream if desired.

S'mores in a Jar

Ingredients

- **1 cup** graham cracker crumbs
- **1 cup** chocolate pudding
- **1 cup** mini marshmallows
- **Chocolate syrup**, for drizzling

Instructions

1. **Layer Ingredients**: In jars, layer graham cracker crumbs, chocolate pudding, and mini marshmallows.
2. **Finish**: Drizzle with chocolate syrup before serving.

Lemon Curd Tart

Ingredients

- **1 pre-baked tart shell**
- **1 cup** lemon juice
- **1 cup** sugar
- **4 large eggs**
- **½ cup** butter, melted
- **Zest of 2 lemons**

Instructions

1. **Mix Filling**: In a bowl, whisk together lemon juice, sugar, eggs, melted butter, and zest.
2. **Bake**: Pour into tart shell and bake at 350°F (175°C) for 20-25 minutes until set. Cool before serving.

Enjoy these delightful desserts!

Pumpkin Cheesecake

Ingredients

- **1 ½ cups** graham cracker crumbs
- **½ cup** sugar
- **½ cup** melted butter
- **2 cups** cream cheese, softened
- **1 cup** pumpkin puree
- **1 cup** sugar
- **3 large eggs**
- **1 tsp** vanilla extract
- **1 tsp** pumpkin pie spice

Instructions

1. **Prepare Crust**: Mix graham cracker crumbs, sugar, and melted butter. Press into a springform pan.
2. **Mix Filling**: In a bowl, beat cream cheese, pumpkin puree, sugar, eggs, vanilla, and spice until smooth.
3. **Bake**: Pour filling into crust and bake at 325°F (160°C) for 50-60 minutes. Cool and refrigerate before serving.

Red Velvet Cake

Ingredients

- **2 ½ cups** all-purpose flour
- **1 ½ cups** sugar
- **1 tsp** baking soda
- **1 tsp** salt
- **1 tsp** cocoa powder
- **1 ½ cups** vegetable oil
- **1 cup** buttermilk
- **2 large eggs**
- **2 tbsp** red food coloring
- **1 tsp** vanilla extract
- **1 tsp** white vinegar

Instructions

1. **Mix Dry Ingredients**: In a bowl, combine flour, sugar, baking soda, salt, and cocoa.
2. **Combine Wet Ingredients**: In another bowl, whisk oil, buttermilk, eggs, food coloring, vanilla, and vinegar.
3. **Combine & Bake**: Mix wet and dry ingredients, then divide into greased cake pans. Bake at 350°F (175°C) for 25-30 minutes. Cool before frosting.

Panna Cotta

Ingredients

- **2 cups** heavy cream
- **½ cup** sugar
- **1 tsp** vanilla extract
- **2 ½ tsp** gelatin
- **3 tbsp** cold water

Instructions

1. **Dissolve Gelatin**: In a small bowl, sprinkle gelatin over cold water and let sit.
2. **Heat Cream**: In a saucepan, heat cream, sugar, and vanilla until sugar dissolves. Remove from heat and stir in gelatin until melted.
3. **Chill**: Pour into molds and refrigerate for at least 4 hours until set. Serve with fruit or sauce.

Apple Crisp

Ingredients

- **4 cups** sliced apples
- **½ cup** sugar
- **1 tsp** cinnamon
- **1 cup** rolled oats
- **¾ cup** flour
- **¾ cup** brown sugar
- **½ cup** butter, softened

Instructions

1. **Prepare Apples**: Toss sliced apples with sugar and cinnamon, then place in a baking dish.
2. **Make Topping**: In a bowl, mix oats, flour, brown sugar, and butter until crumbly. Spread over apples.
3. **Bake**: Bake at 350°F (175°C) for 30-35 minutes until golden. Serve warm.

Peanut Butter Pie

Ingredients

- **1 pre-made graham cracker crust**
- **1 cup** creamy peanut butter
- **1 cup** powdered sugar
- **1 cup** whipped cream
- **Chocolate sauce**, for drizzling

Instructions

1. **Mix Filling**: In a bowl, beat peanut butter and powdered sugar until smooth. Fold in whipped cream.
2. **Fill Crust**: Spoon mixture into the crust and smooth the top.
3. **Chill**: Refrigerate for at least 4 hours. Drizzle with chocolate sauce before serving.

Cheesecake Brownies

Ingredients

- **1 cup** unsweetened cocoa powder
- **1 cup** sugar
- **½ cup** butter, melted
- **2 large eggs**
- **1 tsp** vanilla extract
- **½ cup** flour
- **8 oz** cream cheese, softened
- **¼ cup** sugar
- **1 egg**

Instructions

1. **Prepare Brownie Mix**: In a bowl, mix cocoa, sugar, butter, eggs, vanilla, and flour until combined.
2. **Make Cheesecake Layer**: In another bowl, beat cream cheese, sugar, and egg until smooth.
3. **Layer & Bake**: Pour brownie mix into a greased pan, dollop cheesecake mixture on top, and swirl. Bake at 350°F (175°C) for 25-30 minutes. Cool before cutting.

Berry Trifle

Ingredients

- **2 cups** mixed berries (strawberries, blueberries, raspberries)
- **1 pound** pound cake, cubed
- **2 cups** whipped cream
- **Mint leaves**, for garnish

Instructions

1. **Layer Ingredients**: In a trifle dish, layer cubed pound cake, mixed berries, and whipped cream.
2. **Repeat**: Continue layering until the dish is full. Garnish with mint leaves before serving.

Mocha Pudding

Ingredients

- **1 cup** milk
- **¼ cup** sugar
- **2 tbsp** cocoa powder
- **1 tbsp** instant coffee
- **2 tbsp** cornstarch
- **1 tsp** vanilla extract

Instructions

1. **Combine Dry Ingredients**: In a saucepan, mix sugar, cocoa, instant coffee, and cornstarch.
2. **Add Milk**: Gradually stir in milk and cook over medium heat, stirring until thickened.
3. **Cool & Serve**: Remove from heat, stir in vanilla, and let cool before serving.

Enjoy these delicious desserts!

Coconut Cream Pie

Ingredients

- **1 pre-baked pie crust**
- **1 cup** coconut milk
- **1 cup** heavy cream
- **¾ cup** sugar
- **3 tbsp** cornstarch
- **4 large egg yolks**
- **1 tsp** vanilla extract
- **1 cup** shredded coconut (toasted)
- **Whipped cream**, for topping

Instructions

1. **Make Filling**: In a saucepan, combine coconut milk, heavy cream, sugar, and cornstarch. Cook over medium heat, whisking until thickened. Remove from heat.
2. **Add Egg Yolks**: Temper egg yolks by mixing with a bit of the hot filling, then stir back into the saucepan. Cook for another minute.
3. **Cool & Assemble**: Stir in vanilla and toasted coconut. Pour into the crust and refrigerate until set. Top with whipped cream before serving.

Rice Pudding

Ingredients

- **1 cup** Arborio rice
- **4 cups** milk
- **½ cup** sugar
- **1 tsp** vanilla extract
- **½ tsp** cinnamon
- **Pinch of salt**
- **Raisins** (optional)

Instructions

1. **Cook Rice**: In a saucepan, combine rice, milk, sugar, and salt. Cook over medium heat, stirring frequently, until rice is tender and the mixture thickens (about 20-25 minutes).
2. **Flavor**: Stir in vanilla, cinnamon, and raisins if using. Serve warm or chilled.

Chocolate Chip Cookie Pie

Ingredients

- **1 cup** brown sugar
- **½ cup** granulated sugar
- **1 cup** butter, softened
- **2 large eggs**
- **2 tsp** vanilla extract
- **2 ½ cups** all-purpose flour
- **1 tsp** baking soda
- **½ tsp** salt
- **1 cup** chocolate chips

Instructions

1. **Mix Ingredients**: In a bowl, cream together sugars and butter. Add eggs and vanilla, mixing well. Gradually add flour, baking soda, and salt. Stir in chocolate chips.
2. **Bake**: Pour into a greased pie dish and bake at 350°F (175°C) for 30-35 minutes until golden. Cool before slicing.

Mango Sticky Rice

Ingredients

- **1 cup** glutinous rice
- **1 cup** coconut milk
- **½ cup** sugar
- **2 ripe mangoes**, sliced
- **Sesame seeds** or **mung beans** for garnish

Instructions

1. **Prepare Rice**: Soak rice in water for at least 4 hours or overnight. Drain and steam for about 20-25 minutes until tender.
2. **Make Coconut Sauce**: In a saucepan, heat coconut milk and sugar until dissolved. Reserve some for drizzling.
3. **Serve**: Mix cooked rice with coconut sauce. Serve with mango slices and drizzle with reserved sauce. Garnish with sesame seeds.

Nutella Mousse

Ingredients

- **1 cup** Nutella
- **2 cups** heavy cream
- **1 tsp** vanilla extract

Instructions

1. **Whip Cream**: In a bowl, whip heavy cream until soft peaks form.
2. **Combine**: Gently fold Nutella and vanilla into the whipped cream until fully combined.
3. **Chill**: Refrigerate for at least 2 hours before serving.

Chocolate Lava Cake

Ingredients

- ½ **cup** unsalted butter
- **1 cup** dark chocolate, chopped
- **2 large eggs**
- **2 large egg yolks**
- ½ **cup** sugar
- ¼ **cup** all-purpose flour

Instructions

1. **Melt Chocolate**: In a saucepan, melt butter and chocolate together until smooth.
2. **Mix Eggs**: In a bowl, whisk together eggs, yolks, and sugar. Gradually add melted chocolate, then fold in flour.
3. **Bake**: Pour into greased ramekins and bake at 425°F (220°C) for 12-14 minutes until edges are firm but center is soft. Let cool for 1 minute, then invert to serve.

Banana Pudding

Ingredients

- **2 cups** milk
- **½ cup** sugar
- **⅓ cup** cornstarch
- **1 tsp** vanilla extract
- **4 ripe bananas**
- **1 box** vanilla wafers
- **Whipped cream**, for topping

Instructions

1. **Cook Pudding**: In a saucepan, combine milk, sugar, and cornstarch. Cook over medium heat, stirring until thickened. Remove from heat and stir in vanilla.
2. **Layer**: In a dish, layer pudding, banana slices, and vanilla wafers. Repeat layers and top with whipped cream. Chill before serving.

Carrot Cake

Ingredients

- **2 cups** all-purpose flour
- **2 cups** sugar
- **1 tsp** baking powder
- **1 tsp** baking soda
- **1 tsp** cinnamon
- **1 tsp** salt
- **1 cup** vegetable oil
- **4 large eggs**
- **3 cups** grated carrots
- **1 cup** crushed pineapple, drained
- **½ cup** chopped walnuts (optional)

Instructions

1. **Mix Dry Ingredients**: In a bowl, combine flour, sugar, baking powder, baking soda, cinnamon, and salt.
2. **Combine Wet Ingredients**: In another bowl, whisk oil and eggs. Stir in grated carrots, pineapple, and walnuts.
3. **Combine & Bake**: Mix wet and dry ingredients, pour into greased cake pans, and bake at 350°F (175°C) for 25-30 minutes. Cool before frosting.

Enjoy these delectable desserts!

Matcha Parfait

Ingredients

- **1 cup** Greek yogurt
- **2 tbsp** matcha powder
- **2 tbsp** honey
- **1 cup** granola
- **½ cup** mixed berries

Instructions

1. **Mix Yogurt**: In a bowl, combine Greek yogurt, matcha powder, and honey until smooth.
2. **Layer Ingredients**: In glasses, layer matcha yogurt, granola, and mixed berries. Repeat layers and serve chilled.

Oreo Cheesecake

Ingredients

- **1 ½ cups** crushed Oreo cookies
- **½ cup** butter, melted
- **16 oz** cream cheese, softened
- **1 cup** sugar
- **2 large eggs**
- **1 tsp** vanilla extract
- **½ cup** crushed Oreos (for filling)

Instructions

1. **Prepare Crust**: Mix crushed Oreos with melted butter and press into a springform pan.
2. **Make Filling**: In a bowl, beat cream cheese, sugar, eggs, and vanilla until smooth. Fold in crushed Oreos.
3. **Bake**: Pour filling into the crust and bake at 325°F (160°C) for 55-60 minutes. Chill before serving.

Cherry Clafoutis

Ingredients

- **2 cups** pitted cherries
- **3 large eggs**
- **1 cup** milk
- **¾ cup** sugar
- **1 tsp** vanilla extract
- **½ cup** flour
- **Pinch of salt**

Instructions

1. **Prepare Cherries**: Arrange cherries in a greased baking dish.
2. **Mix Batter**: In a bowl, whisk eggs, milk, sugar, vanilla, flour, and salt until smooth. Pour over cherries.
3. **Bake**: Bake at 350°F (175°C) for 35-40 minutes until puffed and golden. Serve warm.

Almond Joy Parfait

Ingredients

- **1 cup** coconut yogurt
- **½ cup** chocolate granola
- **½ cup** sliced almonds
- **½ cup** shredded coconut
- **Chocolate syrup**, for drizzling

Instructions

1. **Layer Ingredients**: In glasses, layer coconut yogurt, chocolate granola, sliced almonds, and shredded coconut.
2. **Finish**: Drizzle with chocolate syrup and serve chilled.

Tarte Tatin

Ingredients

- **6-8 apples**, peeled and quartered
- **½ cup** butter
- **¾ cup** sugar
- **1 sheet** puff pastry

Instructions

1. **Caramelize Apples**: In an oven-safe skillet, melt butter and sugar until golden. Add apples and cook until slightly softened.
2. **Top with Pastry**: Cover apples with puff pastry and tuck edges in. Bake at 375°F (190°C) for 25-30 minutes until golden.
3. **Invert & Serve**: Let cool for a few minutes, then invert onto a plate and serve warm.

Zucchini Bread Pudding

Ingredients

- **4 cups** cubed day-old bread
- **2 cups** grated zucchini
- **4 large eggs**
- **2 cups** milk
- **¾ cup** sugar
- **1 tsp** vanilla extract
- **1 tsp** cinnamon

Instructions

1. **Prepare Mixture**: In a bowl, whisk eggs, milk, sugar, vanilla, and cinnamon. Stir in zucchini and bread cubes.
2. **Bake**: Pour into a greased baking dish and bake at 350°F (175°C) for 45-50 minutes until set. Serve warm.

Saffron Rice Pudding

Ingredients

- **1 cup** Arborio rice
- **4 cups** milk
- **½ cup** sugar
- **1 tsp** vanilla extract
- **Pinch of saffron threads**

Instructions

1. **Cook Rice**: In a saucepan, combine rice, milk, sugar, and saffron. Cook over medium heat, stirring frequently, until rice is tender and creamy (about 25-30 minutes).
2. **Flavor**: Stir in vanilla and serve warm or chilled.

Snickerdoodle Parfait

Ingredients

- **1 cup** Greek yogurt
- **½ cup** cinnamon sugar
- **1 cup** crumbled snickerdoodle cookies
- **Whipped cream**, for topping

Instructions

1. **Layer Ingredients**: In glasses, layer Greek yogurt, crumbled snickerdoodle cookies, and a sprinkle of cinnamon sugar.
2. **Finish**: Top with whipped cream and a final dusting of cinnamon sugar. Serve chilled.

Enjoy these delightful desserts!

Coconut Macaroon Jars

Ingredients

- **2 ½ cups** shredded coconut
- **1 cup** sweetened condensed milk
- **1 tsp** vanilla extract
- **½ cup** chocolate chips (optional)

Instructions

1. **Mix Ingredients**: In a bowl, combine shredded coconut, sweetened condensed milk, and vanilla until well combined.
2. **Assemble Jars**: Layer the mixture in small jars, adding chocolate chips if desired. Chill for at least 1 hour before serving.

Funfetti Cake

Ingredients

- 2 ½ **cups** all-purpose flour
- 1 ½ **cups** sugar
- **1 cup** butter, softened
- **4 large eggs**
- **1 cup** milk
- **1 tbsp** vanilla extract
- **1 tbsp** baking powder
- **½ cup** rainbow sprinkles

Instructions

1. **Mix Wet Ingredients**: In a bowl, cream together butter and sugar. Add eggs, milk, and vanilla, mixing well.
2. **Combine Dry Ingredients**: In another bowl, whisk flour, baking powder, and sprinkles. Gradually add to the wet mixture.
3. **Bake**: Pour into a greased cake pan and bake at 350°F (175°C) for 30-35 minutes. Cool before frosting.

Chocolate Peanut Butter Pie

Ingredients

- **1 pre-made graham cracker crust**
- **1 cup** creamy peanut butter
- **1 cup** powdered sugar
- **1 cup** heavy cream
- **½ cup** chocolate chips

Instructions

1. **Mix Filling**: In a bowl, beat peanut butter and powdered sugar until smooth. Fold in whipped cream until combined.
2. **Assemble Pie**: Pour filling into the crust. Melt chocolate chips and drizzle over the top. Chill for at least 2 hours before serving.

Fruit Salad with Honey Yogurt

Ingredients

- **4 cups** mixed fresh fruit (berries, melon, kiwi, etc.)
- **1 cup** Greek yogurt
- **2 tbsp** honey
- **1 tsp** vanilla extract

Instructions

1. **Prepare Yogurt**: In a bowl, mix Greek yogurt, honey, and vanilla until smooth.
2. **Assemble Salad**: In a serving bowl, combine mixed fruit and drizzle with honey yogurt before serving.

Mini Pavlova

Ingredients

- **4 large egg whites**
- **1 cup** sugar
- **1 tsp** vinegar
- **1 tsp** cornstarch
- **1 cup** whipped cream
- **Fresh fruit** for topping (berries, kiwi, etc.)

Instructions

1. **Prepare Meringue**: Beat egg whites until stiff peaks form, then gradually add sugar, vinegar, and cornstarch. Pipe onto a baking sheet.
2. **Bake**: Bake at 250°F (120°C) for 1 hour. Cool completely.
3. **Assemble**: Top with whipped cream and fresh fruit before serving.

Chocolate Tart

Ingredients

- **1 ½ cups** chocolate cookie crumbs
- **½ cup** butter, melted
- **1 cup** heavy cream
- **8 oz** dark chocolate, chopped
- **2 large eggs**
- **1 tsp** vanilla extract

Instructions

1. **Prepare Crust**: Mix cookie crumbs and melted butter. Press into a tart pan and refrigerate.
2. **Make Filling**: In a saucepan, heat cream until simmering. Pour over chopped chocolate and let sit, then stir until smooth. Whisk in eggs and vanilla.
3. **Bake**: Pour filling into the crust and bake at 350°F (175°C) for 25-30 minutes. Cool before serving.

Dulce de Leche Flan

Ingredients

- **1 cup** sugar (for caramel)
- **4 large eggs**
- **1 can (14 oz)** sweetened condensed milk
- **1 can (12 oz)** evaporated milk
- **1 tsp** vanilla extract

Instructions

1. **Make Caramel**: In a saucepan, melt sugar until golden and pour into a flan mold.
2. **Mix Ingredients**: Blend eggs, condensed milk, evaporated milk, and vanilla until smooth. Pour over caramel.
3. **Bake**: Place in a water bath and bake at 350°F (175°C) for 50-60 minutes. Chill before serving.

Lemon Blueberry Trifle

Ingredients

- **2 cups** lemon curd
- **2 cups** whipped cream
- **2 cups** blueberries
- **1 store-bought pound cake**, cubed

Instructions

1. **Layer Ingredients**: In a trifle dish, layer cubed pound cake, lemon curd, whipped cream, and blueberries.
2. **Repeat Layers**: Continue layering until the dish is full. Chill before serving.

Enjoy these delicious desserts!

Gingerbread Cake

Ingredients

- **2 ½ cups** all-purpose flour
- **1 tsp** baking soda
- **1 tsp** baking powder
- **1 tsp** ground ginger
- **1 tsp** ground cinnamon
- **½ tsp** ground cloves
- **½ tsp** salt
- **1 cup** unsalted butter, softened
- **1 cup** brown sugar
- **4 large eggs**
- **1 cup** molasses

Instructions

1. **Mix Dry Ingredients**: In a bowl, whisk together flour, baking soda, baking powder, spices, and salt.
2. **Cream Butter and Sugar**: In another bowl, beat butter and brown sugar until fluffy. Add eggs one at a time, then molasses.
3. **Combine & Bake**: Gradually mix dry ingredients into wet. Pour into a greased cake pan and bake at 350°F (175°C) for 30-35 minutes. Cool before serving.

Chocolate Biscotti Parfait

Ingredients

- **1 batch chocolate biscotti**, crumbled
- **2 cups** whipped cream
- **½ cup** chocolate chips
- **Chocolate syrup**, for drizzling

Instructions

1. **Layer Ingredients**: In glasses, layer crumbled biscotti, whipped cream, and chocolate chips.
2. **Finish**: Drizzle with chocolate syrup and repeat layers. Serve chilled.

Blackberry Fool

Ingredients

- **2 cups** blackberries
- **½ cup** sugar
- **1 cup** heavy cream
- **1 tsp** vanilla extract

Instructions

1. **Prepare Blackberries**: In a saucepan, cook blackberries and sugar over medium heat until soft. Let cool.
2. **Whip Cream**: In a bowl, whip heavy cream and vanilla until soft peaks form. Gently fold in the blackberry mixture.
3. **Serve**: Spoon into serving dishes and chill before serving.

Pistachio Pudding

Ingredients

- **1 cup** milk
- **1 cup** heavy cream
- **⅓ cup** sugar
- **3 tbsp** cornstarch
- **½ cup** crushed pistachios
- **1 tsp** vanilla extract

Instructions

1. **Mix Ingredients**: In a saucepan, whisk milk, cream, sugar, and cornstarch. Cook over medium heat, stirring until thickened.
2. **Add Flavor**: Stir in crushed pistachios and vanilla. Pour into serving bowls and chill before serving.

Strawberry Rhubarb Crumble

Ingredients

- **2 cups** sliced rhubarb
- **2 cups** sliced strawberries
- **¾ cup** sugar
- **1 tsp** vanilla extract
- **1 cup** oats
- **½ cup** flour
- **½ cup** brown sugar
- **½ cup** butter, melted

Instructions

1. **Prepare Fruit Filling**: In a bowl, combine rhubarb, strawberries, sugar, and vanilla. Pour into a baking dish.
2. **Make Crumble Topping**: In another bowl, mix oats, flour, brown sugar, and melted butter until crumbly. Sprinkle over the fruit.
3. **Bake**: Bake at 350°F (175°C) for 35-40 minutes until golden and bubbly. Serve warm.

Vanilla Bean Pudding

Ingredients

- **2 cups** milk
- **⅓ cup** sugar
- **2 tbsp** cornstarch
- **1 tsp** vanilla bean paste

Instructions

1. **Combine Ingredients**: In a saucepan, whisk milk, sugar, and cornstarch. Cook over medium heat, stirring until thickened.
2. **Add Vanilla**: Stir in vanilla bean paste and pour into serving dishes. Chill before serving.

Cookie Butter Cups

Ingredients

- **1 cup** cookie butter
- **1 cup** dark chocolate chips
- **¼ cup** crushed cookies (for topping)

Instructions

1. **Melt Chocolate**: In a microwave-safe bowl, melt chocolate chips until smooth.
2. **Assemble Cups**: Line muffin tins with cupcake liners. Spoon melted chocolate into the bottom, add a layer of cookie butter, and top with more chocolate.
3. **Chill**: Sprinkle crushed cookies on top and refrigerate until set.

White Chocolate Raspberry Cheesecake

Ingredients

- **1 ½ cups** graham cracker crumbs
- **½ cup** butter, melted
- **16 oz** cream cheese, softened
- **1 cup** sugar
- **3 large eggs**
- **1 cup** white chocolate, melted
- **1 cup** raspberry puree

Instructions

1. **Prepare Crust**: Mix graham cracker crumbs and melted butter. Press into a springform pan.
2. **Make Filling**: Beat cream cheese and sugar until smooth. Add eggs one at a time, then melted white chocolate and raspberry puree.
3. **Bake**: Pour filling into the crust and bake at 325°F (160°C) for 50-60 minutes. Cool before serving.

Enjoy these delightful desserts!

Chai-Spiced Rice Pudding

Ingredients

- **1 cup** Arborio rice
- **4 cups** milk
- **½ cup** sugar
- **1 tsp** vanilla extract
- **2-3 chai tea bags** (or 1 tbsp loose chai tea)
- **½ tsp** ground cinnamon
- **¼ tsp** ground cardamom
- **¼ tsp** ground ginger
- **Pinch of salt**

Instructions

1. **Infuse Milk**: In a saucepan, heat milk and add chai tea bags. Let steep for 10-15 minutes, then remove the bags.
2. **Cook Rice**: Add rice, sugar, cinnamon, cardamom, ginger, and salt to the milk. Cook over medium heat, stirring frequently, until the rice is tender and the mixture is creamy (about 25-30 minutes).
3. **Finish**: Stir in vanilla extract. Serve warm or chilled, garnished with additional cinnamon or nuts if desired.

Chocolate Almond Torte

Ingredients

- **8 oz** dark chocolate, chopped
- **½ cup** unsalted butter
- **¾ cup** sugar
- **3 large eggs**
- **½ cup** almond flour
- **1 tsp** vanilla extract
- **Pinch of salt**
- **Powdered sugar**, for dusting

Instructions

1. **Melt Chocolate**: In a saucepan, melt dark chocolate and butter over low heat until smooth. Remove from heat and let cool slightly.
2. **Combine Ingredients**: In a bowl, whisk together sugar and eggs until combined. Stir in the melted chocolate mixture, then add almond flour, vanilla, and salt. Mix until smooth.
3. **Bake**: Pour into a greased round cake pan and bake at 350°F (175°C) for 25-30 minutes. The center should be set but still fudgy. Cool before dusting with powdered sugar and serving.

Enjoy these delicious treats!

www.ingramcontent.com/pod-product-compliance
Lightning Source LLC
LaVergne TN
LVHW081336060526
838201LV00055B/2673